DATE DUE

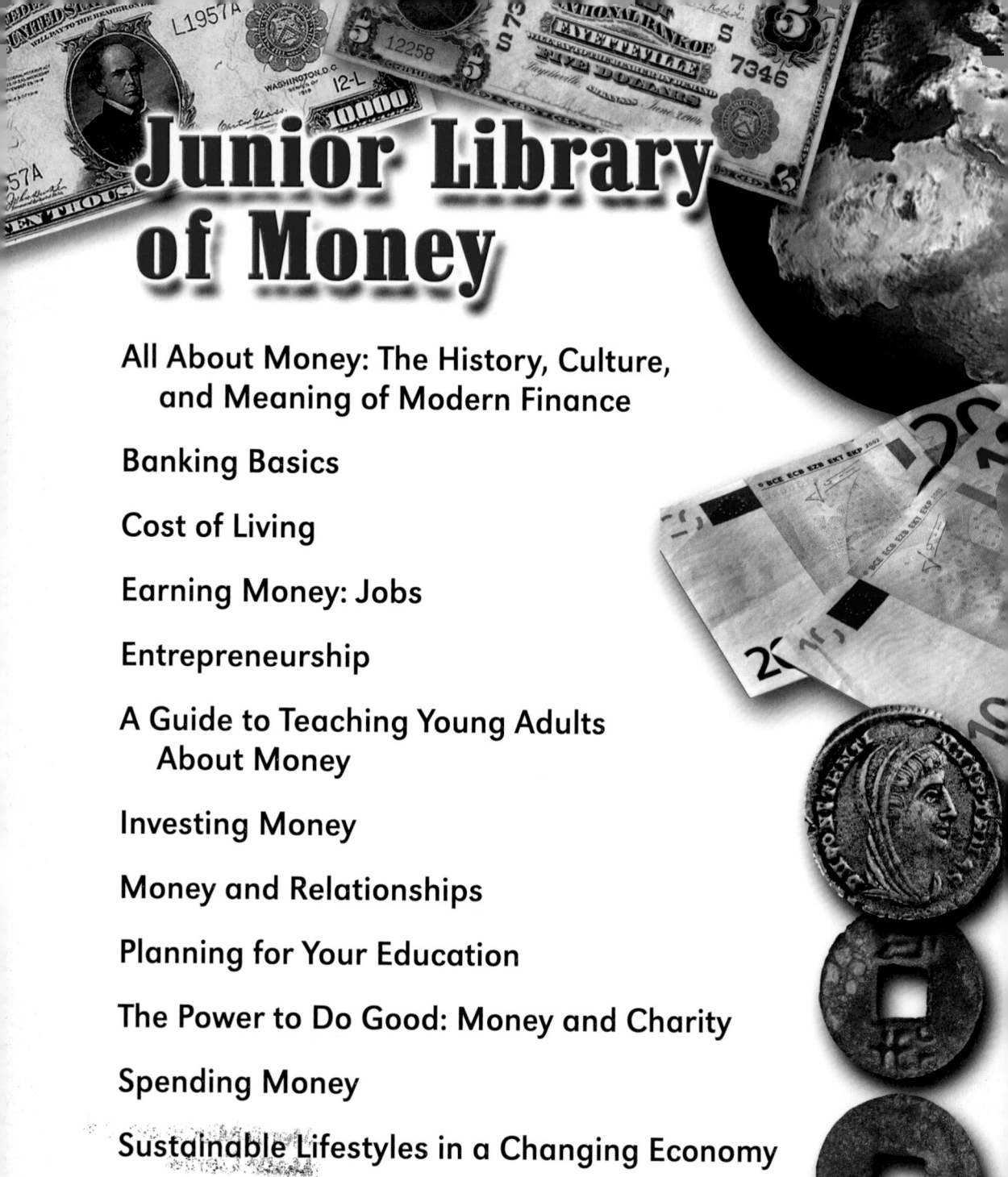

Junior Library of Money

UNDERSTANDING CREDIT

by Helen Thompson

MASON CREST PUBLISHERS INC.
370 Reed Road
Broomall, Pennsylvania 19008
(866)MCP-BOOK (toll free)
www.masoncrest.com

First Printing
9 8 7 6 5 4 3 2 1

Library of Congress Cataloging-in-Publication Data
Thompson, Helen, 1957–
 Understanding credit / by Helen Thompson.
    p. cm.
 Includes bibliographical references and index.
 ISBN 978-1-4222-1772-6 (hbk.)   ISBN 978-1-4222-1759-7 (series)
 ISBN 978-1-4222-1891-4 (pbk.)   ISBN 978-1-4222-1878-5 (pbk. series)
 1. Credit—Juvenile literature. 2. Loans—Juvenile literature. 3. Money—Juvenile literature.
I. Title.
 HG3701.T46 2011
 332.7—dc22
                        2010027891

Design by Wendy Arakawa.
Produced by Harding House
Publishing Service, Inc.
www.hardinghousepages.com
Cover design by Torque
Advertising and Design.
Printed by Bang
Printing.

Contents

Introduction

Our lives interact with the global financial system on an almost daily basis: we take money out of an ATM machine, we use a credit card to go shopping at the mall, we write a check to pay the rent, we apply for a loan to buy a new car, we set something aside in a savings account, we hear on the evening news whether the stock market went up or down. These interactions are not just frequent, they are consequential. Deciding whether to attend college, buying a house, or saving enough for retirement, are decisions with large financial implications for almost every household. Even small decisions like using a debit or a credit card become large when made repeatedly over time.

And yet, many people do not understand how to make good financial decisions. They do not understand how inflation works or why it matters. They do not understand the long-run costs of using consumer credit. They do not understand how to assess whether attending college makes sense, or whether or how much money they should borrow to do so. They do not understand the many different ways there are to save and invest their money and which investments make the most sense for them.

And because they do not understand, they make mistakes. They run up balances they cannot afford to repay on their credit card. They drop out of high school and end up unemployed or trying to make ends meet on a minimum wage job, or they borrow so much to pay for college that they are drowning in debt when they graduate. They don't save enough. They pay high interests rates and fees when lower cost options are available. They don't buy insurance to protect themselves from financial risks. They find themselves declaring bankruptcy, with their homes in foreclosure.

We can do better. We must do better. In an increasingly

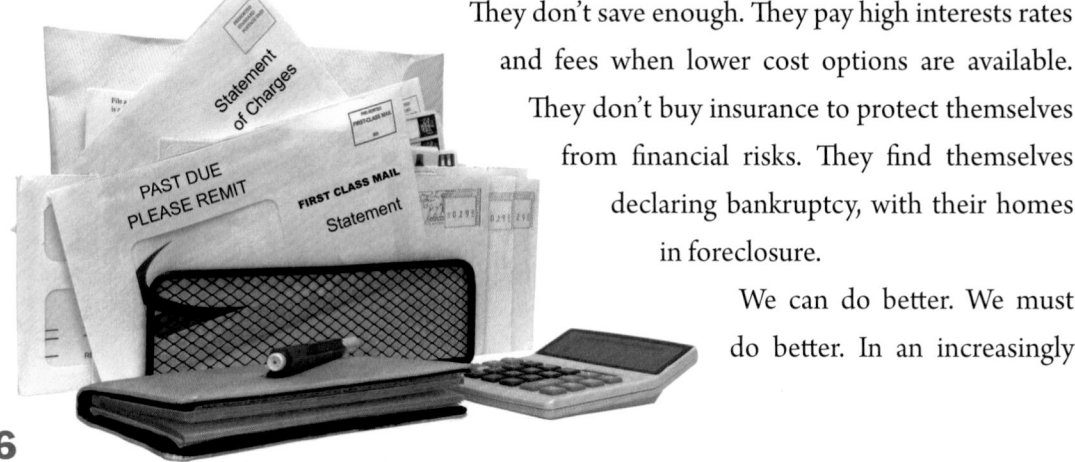

sophisticated financial world, everyone needs a basic knowledge of our financial system. The books in this series provide just such a foundation. The series has individual books devoted specifically to the financial decisions most relevant to children: work, school, and spending money. Other books in the series introduce students to the key institutions of our financial system: money, banks, the stock market, the Federal Reserve, the FDIC. Collectively they teach basic financial concepts: inflation, interest rates, compounding, risk vs. reward, credit ratings, stock ownership, capitalism. They explain how basic financial transactions work: how to write a check, how to balance a checking account, what it means to borrow money. And they provide a brief history of our financial system, tracing how we got where we are today.

There are benefits to all of us of having today's children more financially literate. First, if we can help the students of today start making wise financial choices when they are young, they can hopefully avoid the financial mishaps that have been so much in the news of late. Second, as the financial crisis of 2007–2010 has shown, poor individual financial choices can sometimes have implications for the health of the overall financial system, something that affects everyone. Finally, the financial system is an important part of our overall economy. The students of today are the business and political leaders of tomorrow. We need financially literate citizens to choose the leaders who will guide our economy through the inevitable changes that lie ahead.

Brigitte Madrian, Ph.D.
Aetna Professor of Public
Policy and Corporate
Management
Harvard Kennedy School

7

What is CREDIT?

Have you ever borrowed money from your parents or friends? Maybe you wanted a new bike and couldn't afford it on your own, so you had your parents pay for some of the cost of the bike. Maybe you wanted a snack but didn't have the money, so your friend gave you her change. They might have made an agreement with you. "If I give you this money now," they might've said, "you have to promise you'll pay me back." This agreement is very similar to the way credit works: you borrow money from a bank or company, and promise to pay the money back in the future.

Credit is money you can borrow that you must pay back later. By borrowing money, in the form of a car loan or credit card, for example, you are agreeing that, while you may not have the money to pay the loan back now, you'll have the money in the future, allowing you to pay back the loan then. In many cases, the person who is borrowing the money will have to pay the lender back over time, making payments each month, for instance.

When you borrow money, but wait to pay it back, the amount you owe is called **debt**. Debt can become dangerous, particularly if you let it build up by borrowing money, by using credit, but not paying back those who lent you money. One way that debt can grow is through **interest**. Interest is a percentage of the money you owe, your debt, that is added onto the total amount of money you need to pay back every so often (either by the year or every few months, usually). If you don't pay your debts, they can add up over time, making it more and more difficult to pay them in the future. This means that you must always consider the balance between spending, borrowing, and paying down your debts, in order to be on top of your finances.

Credit comes in many different forms. Auto loans, money borrowed from a bank that is to be spent on buying a car, are a form of credit. Student loans, money borrowed in order to attend college, are also a form of credit. Credit cards are one of the most common types of credit. A credit card lets you borrow money up to a certain amount, beyond which you cannot borrow. You must pay back the money you spend on your credit card each month. Any money that you borrow and agree to pay back in the future or over time can be considered credit. Using credit or getting loans can really help in times of need—but rely on credit too heavily, and you can find yourself deep in debt and having a harder time. Credit is a financial tool you have, but it has to be used wisely in order for you to get the most use out of it without it harming your finances in the long-term.

Why Do You Need Credit?

People need credit for many different reasons. You might rely on credit if you didn't have enough money to make a big purchase. For instance, if you wanted to buy a car, which is a very expensive item, you may need to ask a bank for a car loan. This is a form of credit. You borrow the money you need for part or all of the cost of the car, and then pay your debt down over time. In order to make many large purchases, many of which would be too expensive to pay for all at once, you may need the help of credit. Credit cards can also be of use in an emergency, when you don't have money for something you need right now, perhaps repairs on the car you bought. If you don't have the cash right now, but know you'll have it by the end of the month, you might put a purchase on your credit card to help get you through for a short time.

It's also important to know that the way you use credit (how much you borrow, how soon you pay it back, and a variety of other factors) is used in some cases to judge whether or not you are a good borrower. Using your credit history, banks that you are asking for a loan can see if you paid your debts off on time or if you let them pile up, if you pay your bills each month or if you pay them late, and other measures of how good a borrower you are. If you're looking to get another credit card, credit card companies can use your credit history to evaluate you. This credit history follows you everywhere, and is very important when you want to make larger purchases, such as a car or house, that may require you take out a loan. Building a credit history is one of the reasons you'll need credit. In order to build up a good credit history, you'll need to use credit, either in the form of borrowing money from a bank, or, more commonly, using a credit card, making sure to make payments on your debt on time and in full. Though it may seem odd, using credit is the only way to build a credit history, allowing you to use more credit and get better loans when you need to make larger purchases in the future. This means almost everyone who wants to buy a house, buy a car, or send their kids to college, will need to use credit at some point, if only to add to their credit history.

DIFFERENT KINDS OF CREDIT

Credit can come in many different forms. Each involves, at the most basic level, borrowing money and paying it back over time.

Here are a few commonly used kinds of credit:

- Auto loans
- Student loans
- Credit cards
- **Mortgages**

With each of these kinds of credit, the borrower must pay down the debt that they owe the lender. The cost of these kinds of credit may differ, but the way that the costs are calculated are often similar. The cost of credit does not include the amount of money that has been borrowed. Instead, the cost is money that the borrower must pay in addition to the money that she borrowed (which, of course, must also be paid back). Credit cost comes in the form of interest and, in some cases, optional fees that cover services like credit **insurance**.

CAR LOANS

Car loans, also called auto loans, are some of the most common loans that **consumers** need. Given by banks and other financial insititutions, or set-up by car dealers, car loans are simply another form of credit. As is the case with any kind of credit, when you take out a car loan, you are agreeing to pay back the amount of the loan, as well as any additional costs (such as interest on the loan). Car loans are only to be used to purchase a new or used car, nothing else.

Car loans help people pay for what is one of the largest purchase they'll make in their lives. In fact, it's because cars are often so expensive that car loans, as well as many other kinds of credit, exist. It would be difficult to walk to the car dealership and pay for a car in cash, all at once. Car loans make it possible to buy a car and then make payments on that car over time, meaning that people don't need to have all of the cost of a car when making the purchase. Car loans put a large purchase like a car in the reach of the average person.

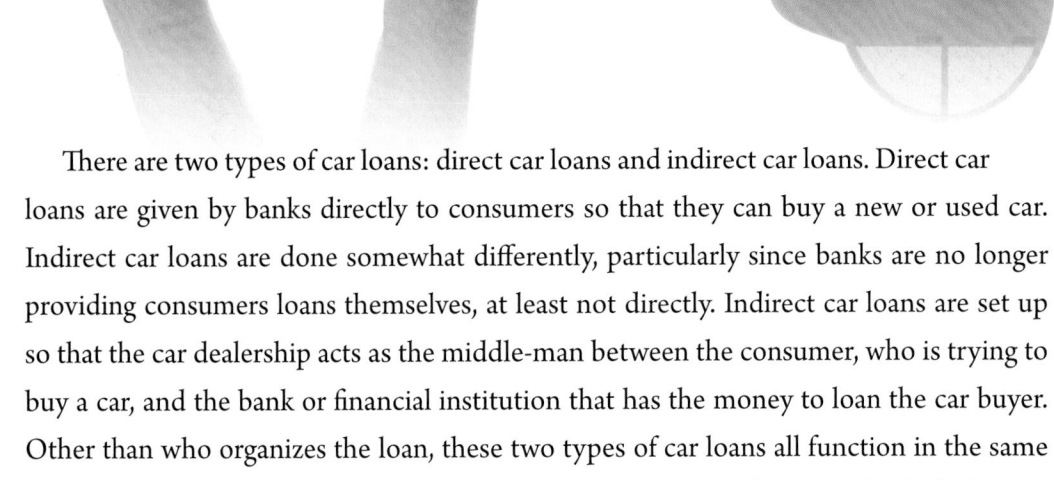

Before approving a car loan, lenders usually check the credit history of the borrower to make sure he is likely to pay his debts in a timely way. This is another reason why credit is so important, as it can mean the difference between being approved or rejected for a car loan.

There are two types of car loans: direct car loans and indirect car loans. Direct car loans are given by banks directly to consumers so that they can buy a new or used car. Indirect car loans are done somewhat differently, particularly since banks are no longer providing consumers loans themselves, at least not directly. Indirect car loans are set up so that the car dealership acts as the middle-man between the consumer, who is trying to buy a car, and the bank or financial institution that has the money to loan the car buyer. Other than who organizes the loan, these two types of car loans all function in the same way from the point of view of the borrower, who is responsible for paying back the loan in full, in addition to any interest or extra costs that are included with her debt.

STUDENT LOANS

Today, college can cost tens of thousands of dollars per year. Just as car loans make cars, expensive as they are, affordable for those who can't pay for them all at once, student loans put high-quality, though pricey, education within the grasp of more students. Student loans, like car loans, are given by banks or other financial institutions. These organizations lend money to students who are looking to attend college or university, making that dream more managable from a financial perspective. In most cases, students don't have to make payments on their debts until after they have graduated from college. It's also possible, with many loans, to **defer** payment—to put off making payments on the debt until the borrowing student is more able to make regular payments (though students can't do this forever). As is the case with all kinds of credit, interest is also added to the amount that students must pay. Though private banks and companies make many student loans, the U.S. government also offers some loans for students attending college.

CREDIT CARDS

Credit cards are one of the most used forms of credit. Offered by banks or credit card companies, credit cards allow the people who have them to make purchases using their cards, and then pay for them later. Banks and credit card companies set a cap on the amount of money a person can spend using the card, called a credit limit. Each credit card user has his own credit limit. Unlike debit cards, which draw funds from bank accounts that contain cash, credit cards are based on using borrowed money to pay for purchases, and then paying back that amount each month.

Credit cards are often good for emergencies, when you need to pay for something but don't have the cash on hand. Putting purchases on your credit card is fine as long as you make sure to regularly pay off the purchases you've made. If you use your credit card to buy many things but don't pay off your debt, you may harm your credit history.

Remember, credit cards don't draw on money you actually have. Instead, they draw on money you promise you'll have in the future. Credit cards aren't a license to spend more, and certainly not an invitation to spend money you don't have. You must pay off all the money you spend using your credit card, if not now, then in the future. The best way to use credit cards, particularly when just starting out, is to make only certain purchases using your card, and then make regular payments to your credit-card debt, making sure to keep your debt as low as you can.

MORTGAGES

A mortgage, also sometimes called a mortgage loan, is a loan you can get in order to help pay for a house. Just as is the case with credit cards, auto loans, and other forms of credit, mortgages are offered by banks or other financial institutions. In the same way car loans can be organized directly or indirectly, mortgages can be set up by the bank offering the loan directly, or they can be set up by **intermediaries**, in the same way car dealers are able to set up loans for buyers.

A few key differences between mortgages and other loans make mortgages unique. First, mortgages, because they are loans covering the purchase of real estate, one of the largest purchases people make in their lives, are often paid off over the course of many years. Most mortgages come with a payment plan, complete with a timeline for making payments. These timelines can span up to thirty years, making mortgage payments a long-term financial commitment.

Another way in which mortgages are a unique form of credit is the way that lenders are able to take a borrower's house if she does not meet the requirements of the mortgage, such as the timeline by which she must make payments. This is called foreclosure or repossesion. If a borrower (in this case known as the mortgager) agrees to pay a lender (in this case called the mortgagee) in a certain amount of time, but fails to do so, he can have his house **foreclosed** on. In this case, the bank owns the house that was paid for by the money they loaned out, and the bank must sell the house itself in order to make back what is owed. This is the main difference between a mortgage and any other type of loan.

Mortgages allow people who might not have enough money to pay for a house themselves, to borrow the money they need to make the purchase, and then pay off debt over the course of years. This puts the dream of owning a house within reach for many more families and individuals than could pay for their homes on their own, without the help of credit. Like all forms of credit, however, everything depends on the borrower paying the lender on time and in full.

OTHER LOANS

Auto loans, mortgages, and student loans aren't the only kinds of loans you can get. Though these three are most likely the largest loans you would ever need to take out, many people also take out a variety of smaller loans. Many of these kinds of loans, however, aren't set up in the same way as larger loans. Some of these loans are given out by companies that are not banks.

First of all, remember that your credit card is a sort of loan. Credit-card debt is technically money you have been lent by a bank or credit card company to make purchases. Paying down your credit card balance is very much the same as making payments on loan debt. Thinking of credit as a loan can be a good way of understanding the importance of keeping down the amount you owe on your cards.

If you have a debit card that is linked to your checking account, and you use more money than your account holds, your bank will usually charge you what is called an **overdraft** fee. This fee is actually a type of loan, since the fee is charged to your card when you have no money in your account. Your account balance may even be a negative number, meaning you not only have no money in your account, but that you must also pay the bank back the amount you have overdrawn your account in addition to the amount charged to you in the form of the overdraft fee.

Another type of small loan that you can take out is called a payday loan. These types of loans are based around the idea of you getting paycheck money ahead of time. In order to get a payday loan, you must agree that you will pay a percentage of the money you get in your paycheck to the lender. The companies that give out payday loans are not banks. Payday loans may seem like a great idea at the time you're getting the loan, but often these kinds of deals result in a cycle of debt that is difficult to escape. You may get your paycheck early, but you won't get all of it. These short-term loans often have very high interest rates as well, meaning you may end up paying much more than you had planned if you pay late, even by a day. Payday loans are a particularly risky way to borrow money. Of course, all loans carry with them a certain amount of risk, since you are borrowing and using money you plan to pay back in the future. Always make sure you know exactly what you're getting and what you are agreeing to whenever you get a loan.

GOOD, BAD,& NONEXISTENT CREDIT

Now that you know what credit is and are aware of a few of the different kinds of credit available, you need to know another way in which people talk about credit. You might have heard someone refer to good or bad credit. When someone says this, he is talking about, essentially, credit history; that is, the record of whether or not a borrower made payments on her debt on time, whether she let debts grow, and, generally, how she used her credit. If you have good credit, that means you have a good credit history. Your record is one of paying bills on time, making sure your credit cards are paid off each month, and always keeping track of how much you owe. Bad credit means your credit history is less than good, meaning you've not paid off your debts in a timely way and you've kept the amount you owe on credit cards high. It's also possible to have no credit at all (if you never borrow money or hold a credit card, you cannot build a credit history). Whether you have good credit, bad credit, or no credit can affect your ability to get loans and credit cards.

GOOD CREDIT

Having good credit means that you pay off your debts completely and always on time. If you have good credit, banks and other lenders will feel better about lending you money or giving you a credit card.

NON-EXISTENT CREDIT

Many students simply have no credit. This means that they have yet to get a credit card or borrow money from a bank or other lender. Having no credit means there is no record of your credit history.

BAD CREDIT

If you have bad credit, you've not paid off your debts on time. A poor credit history can build up as a result of using credit cards too much while letting debts grow. Bad credit makes it harder for lenders to give you loans in the future.

Building Good Credit

Building good credit can be done in many different ways. There are many actions that affect your credit history, and though each may be small, they all add up to giving lenders a sense of how good a borrower you are. Remember, your credit history is a reflection of you and how you use credit, so if you improve your credit habits, your history will reflect that. Likewise, if you start using credit and not paying your debts, that information will become part of your credit history as well. First, in order to build good credit you should always make sure to pay all of your bills on time.

Opening a checking or savings account can be another great way to build good credit. If you have a credit card, make sure to always pay off your debt. Keeping your credit card **balance**, the amount of money you owe, to a minimum is the best way to use your credit card to build good credit. Applying for a credit card with the lowest interest rate you can find is also good for your credit.

A NONTRADITIONAL CREDIT HISTORY

Electricity bill

778 300

22

Building your credit history can be difficult, especially for young people who are just starting to think about credit. In addition, young people may not want to take out a loan or get a credit card. Getting a loan or using a credit card can be a big responsibility, because the borrower must always pay back what he borrows.

If you don't want to get a loan or use a credit card to build your credit history, you can build what is called a nontradtional credit history. To create this nontraditional credit history, you must first make sure to pay all your bills on time. This includes rent and utility bills, as well as bills for telephone or Internet service. Try to keep copies of any checks you write, so that you can prove that you made on-time payments if need be. Last, you can ask for a reference letter from your landlord, from the company who provides your utilities, or your telephone and Internet service provider. This letter can describe the length of time during which you paid your bills on time and in full. Together, these items can be used as evidence of your credit history, even without a credit card or loan.

MANAGING YOUR CREDIT

Managing your credit may seem overwhelming, but by taking a few simple steps, you can keep track of your debts and prevent them from growing beyond what you are able to pay.

Keeping track of the money you spend is the first step toward managing your credit. Keeping a money journal or holding onto receipts is a great way to do this. After you know how much you're spending and on what, make a **budget**. Sticking to that budget will allow you even greater control over your spending. Make sure not to charge big purchases either, instead saving up for them over time. As always, keep the balances on your credit card low.

BUDGET

MORTGAGE........$ 1500.00
CAR LEASE.............249.00
CAR INS....................85.00
HOUSE PHONE..........65.00
...NE.........39.00
.................545.00
...............39.00
...............35.00
NS.............375.00
HEALTH INS............400.00
GROCERIES..............300.00
VACATIONS...............400.00
ENTER INMENT....350.00
MISC.....................

What's a
CREDIT REPORT?

Credit Report

Each time you use your credit card, make a payment on a debt, or miss a payment altogether, that information is recorded on your credit report. Your credit report is a way of looking at your credit history. It reflects how you use credit and how you pay off your debts. Lenders often rely on looking at a potential borrower's credit report in order to see whether or not he is likely to pay off his debts. Your credit report contains a wide variety of information lenders might consider important. This includes basic information like your name, your present and past home addresses, and the names of employers for whom you've worked. It also includes information about your debts and your payment history for loans and credit cards. Any information regarding **bankruptcy** that lenders may need to make decisions on loans or credit cards is also included in your credit report.

DID YOU KNOW?

It's also important to know what's NOT included in your credit report. Your credit report will not hold any information on your race, gender, ethnicity, religion, nationality or marital status. Only financial information is included.

What's a Credit Score?

Your credit report isn't all that banks and other lenders use to assess whether or not you're a responsible borrower. They also often examine potential borrowers' credit scores. A credit score is a number calculated by using a variety of information about how a borrower uses credit, and how effective she is at paying off her debts. This number, along with your credit report, helps lenders decide whether you are a person they should give a loan.

In 1958, the Fair Issac Corporation (commonly called FICO for short) created the first method for calculating credit score. Twelve years later, in 1970, it applied that method to determining the credit score of individuals seeking a bank credit card. Today, several different companies (called credit bureaus) calculate credit scores. It's possible, because more than one credit bureau exists (and each uses a slightly different method of calculating credit scores), to have more than one credit score.

Your credit score is a number between 300 and 850, though most scores (60 percent) fall between 650 and 799. The median (average) credit score is 690 to 740. A score above 700 is considered to be high. A score between 580 and 619 is considered low.

EXP 12/12

How is a person's credit score determined? Using five main factors, FICO, or one of the other credit bureaus, calculates credit scores. Credit bureaus use these five factors to reach their scores:

1. Payment history: How well have you kept up with credit-card payments? Utility bills? Have you stuck to your loan repayment plans? Your payment history is a reflection of your ability to pay back lenders on time and maintain regular payments for rent, utilities, and phone services.

2. Amounts owed: Do you have any debts that have not been paid off? Before giving you a loan or a credit card, lenders will want to know how much money you already owe on other debts. As a result, this is factored into your credit score.

3. Length of credit history: How long have you been using credit cards or taking out loans? Your credit score incorporates information about how long you've used credit, as well as how you've used it.

4. New credit: Have you been applying for new credit cards recently? Are you actively seeking new loans? If so, these things may damage your credit score, particularly if you're already in debt.

5. Types of credit used: Have you only ever used a single credit card? What kinds of loans have you taken out? Student loans? Auto loans? This information is also used by credit bureaus to determine your credit score.

Taken along with your credit report and additional personal information (such as employment history, the amount you have in savings, and other items) your credit score is a key part of getting new loans or low interest rates on new credit cards.

Check It Out

Once you've built up a credit history, it's best to take a look at your credit report every year. This way, you can keep track of what lenders will see when they are deciding whether or not to give you a loan or a credit card.

In your credit report, you can see your debt payment history and check out how much you owe. Credit reports contain information about how you use your credit cards and store charge cards, as well as information about any student, auto, or home loans you've taken out. Examining your credit report can help you understand where you stand with lenders and **creditors**.

In addition to allowing you to get the edge in planning out your finances, looking at your credit report at least once per year is important because your credit report may contain errors or incorrect information. Finding any kind of error on your credit report isn't a terrible thing; mistakes happen, so it's best to find inaccuracies and correct them, which is a relatively easy process.

With credit reports being so important to your financial future, it's a good thing they are so easy to check. There are a couple different ways you can get a copy of your credit report, some of which are free and some of which will require that you pay a fee before getting your credit report.

You can get one free copy of your credit report each year online at www.annualcreditreport.com. This website is sponsored by three credit bureaus that allow you to purchase additional copies of your credit report (beyond the single free copy you are allowed yearly). Equifax, Experian, and TransUnion, the three main credit reporting companies, allow individuals to buy copies of their credit reports whenever they need. Each of these three companies will provide a slightly different credit report, but, for the most part, these reports contain the same information.

Remember, your credit report contains much of the information that lenders will look at when deciding whether or not you are a responsible borrower. Knowing what information they are seeing can help you stay on top of your credit and debt.

What If There's a Mistake?

If there's a mistake on your credit report, or on a credit card statement—the monthly report of your credit card spending and debt—you can **dispute** anything on your report or statement. It's entirely possible that there's been a simple mistake, resulting in incorrect or inaccurate information. Keep in mind that YOU are responsible for correcting any mistakes you notice in your credit report or statements, especially because no one else will have access to as much information about your credit history as you do. You must dispute any problems you see yourself.

You can usually do your dispute online, on the same sites where you get your credit rating. If you can't do it online, make sure to submit your dispute in writing. Many credit card statements contain an address to which all disputes must be sent. Keep checking the credit bureau to see if and when the error is removed from your credit report.

The Fair Credit Billing Act requires that any credit card statement disputes be sent to the credit card company within 60 days of receiving

DID YOU KNOW?

the billing statement that contains the error. Under the law, disputes must also be submitted in writing.

Why Does It Matter?

Having good credit matters because it can help you get the things you want in your life. At the very least, most people will need to take out loans in order to buy a house or car. Before you can get each of these kinds of loans, home and auto, lenders will look at your credit report and examine your credit history. Using these methods of evaluating how good a borrower you are—how much money you owe, how quickly you are paying it back, how you use your credit cards—lenders make their decisions as to whether they should lend you money.

A high credit score and clean credit history can help you get a loan for a house in the future. You'll likely need to take out a loan to buy cars. It's these kinds of purchasing decisions, decisions that many consider a part of growing up, that make credit so important. You often need to have a credit history in order to access the kinds of loans that can assist you in making these sorts of big decisions.

Down the road, you might also want to use credit to get other kinds of short-term loans that allow you to take advantage of opportunities for which you may not have immediate funds. For example, you have an opportunity to travel to Europe this spring—but you won't be able to pay for the trip until after you get paid for the extra work you're doing this summer. Using credit in this way can allow you to go on the trip—so long as you make sure you really can pay the money back as planned!

The way credit works may seem kind of odd to you. Technically, you need to build up some debt, even if only in the form of a credit card balance that you pay off monthly, in order to build your credit history. Building this credit history is one of the only ways to have access to the kinds of loans you may need for larger purchases.

Remember, you are in control of your credit history. If you have bad credit, you can change it, improving your credit over time. Credit isn't meant to be scary, intimidating, or overwhelming, and it isn't meant to run your life. You are meant to use credit in the ways that best help you live the kind of life you want to lead. Your credit report and credit score don't define who you are, but they are a reflection of the way you use your money. They also aren't ever a final assessment of your credit. They are a snapshot of your credit as it stands now and as it has been in the past. Your credit score can be raised, and your report improved.

By understanding credit, and taking steps toward getting good credit and keeping it, you are taking control of your financial future, ensuring that you'll be ahead of the game when it comes to making important decisions about loans, credit, and debt. It's never too early to start managing your money effectively, and never too late to try and turn your finances around. Making sure your credit stays good is the best way to avoid credit becoming a burden rather than a helpful financial tool.

Protecting Your Credit: PAYING YOUR BILLS

Paying your bills on time and in full is one of the best ways to build good credit, and maintain good credit once you've got it. Remember, your payment history—including utility bill payments, rent, and debt payments—help to determine your credit score, so keeping up with bill payments can have a large effect on your ability to get loans or credit cards. In fact, FICO weights payment history to account for 35 percent of your credit score, the most of any single factor. In addition, paying your credit card bills is vital. Making sure to pay your bills as they come in is an important part of building and protecting good credit. Letting bills pile up can do serious damage to your credit!

Protecting Your Credit: BUDGETING

One of the best ways to make sure you are entirely in charge of your credit card use and debt repayment is to make and keep to a budget. A budget is a way to divide up the money you make ahead of time, so that you can plan and keep track of your spending.

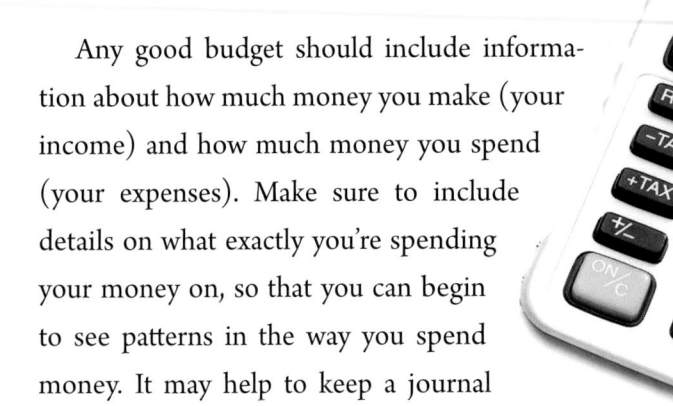

Any good budget should include information about how much money you make (your income) and how much money you spend (your expenses). Make sure to include details on what exactly you're spending your money on, so that you can begin to see patterns in the way you spend money. It may help to keep a journal in which you write down every purchase you make. This journal can give you a good idea of how you spend your money, knowledge you can bring into your budget-making process. Once you've nailed down your spending habits, it's important to next identify your spending **priorities**. These might include rent, bill payments, or debt payments—the sorts of things you must spend money on no matter what. With information on both the amount you're spending, and where you are spending that money, you can begin to better understand how much can go toward paying off debts, keeping your credit score high. Once you're sure of how much money you are able to pay off on your credit card and loan repayments each month, you're less likely to overspend on other things, allowing you to stick more closely to your payment plans. In addition, budgeting is simply a good way to remain in control of your personal finances.

If you need help creating your first budget, there are many ways of getting this kind of assistance. Your public library can be a good place to start, for instance. You can find many resources that can help you plan your budget, and add to your own knowledge of finances. In addition, researching budget creation online can be another good way to get free help with budgeting. Financial professionals can also give you guidance when it comes to creating a budget. Many local community groups sponsor programs that connect budget experts with individuals who need help. These sorts of organizations can make sure you understand how to budget your money effectively. Don't be afraid to ask for help. Keeping track of your money is an important skill you'll need for the rest of your life!

WHAT'S IDENTITY THEFT?

It may sound strange, but it's possible to have your identity stolen. This means that someone has taken your personal and financial information and is using it for himself. Your credit card may have been taken and used, along with information that someone knows about you, to make purchases online, or even take money from your savings account with a stolen ATM card and PIN number. Having your identity stolen simply means someone has enough information about you to pretend that she is you for the purposes of buying things, taking money, or making false documents. For instance, if you see suspicious activity on your monthly credit card bill, you may have had your information stolen. Make sure to contact the authorities, as well as all your creditors and lenders if you suspect identity theft.

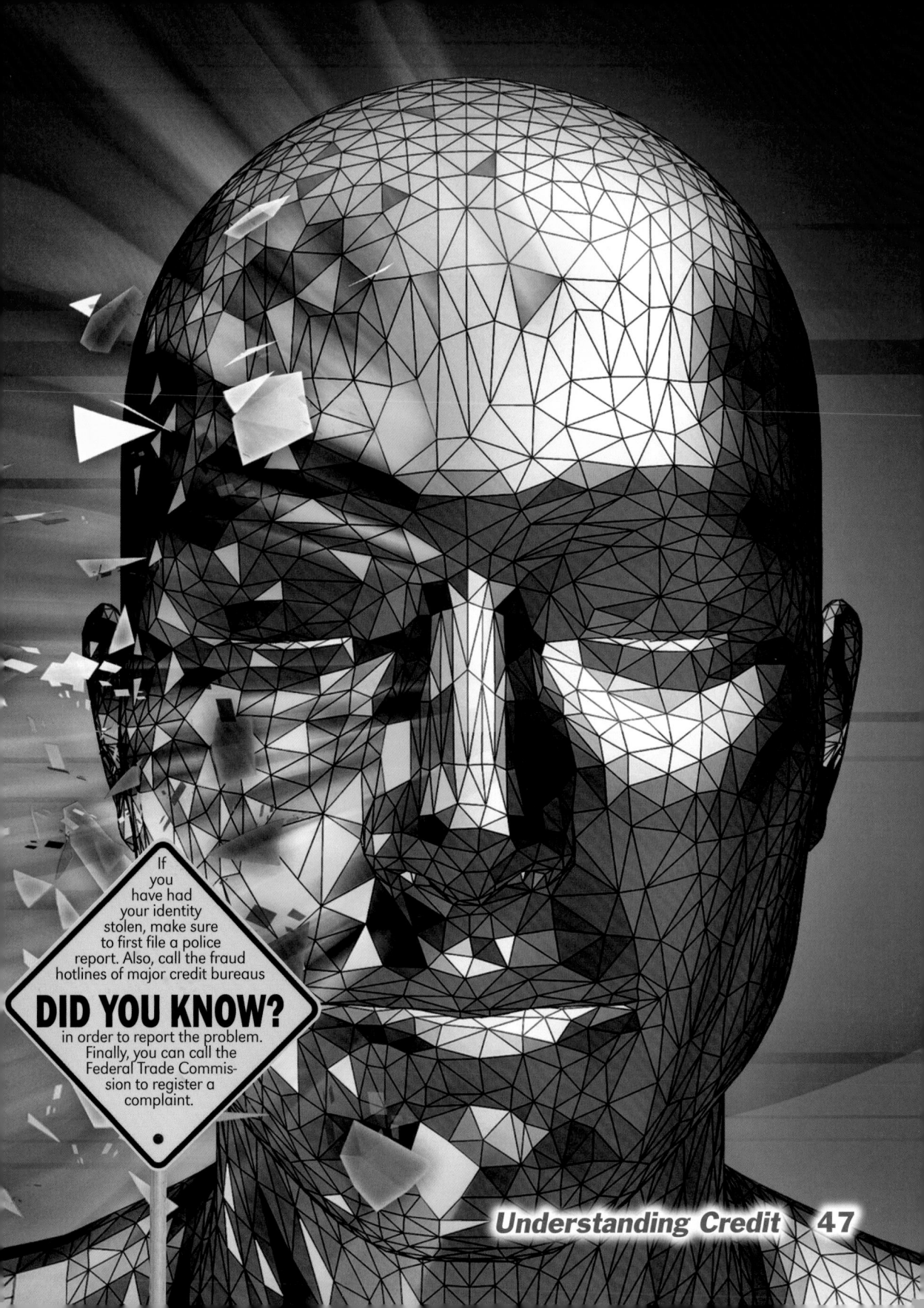

DID YOU KNOW?

If you have had your identity stolen, make sure to first file a police report. Also, call the fraud hotlines of major credit bureaus in order to report the problem. Finally, you can call the Federal Trade Commission to register a complaint.

THE DANGERS OF CREDIT

Credit can be a powerful financial tool, allowing you to make large purchases and manage your money more effectively. It can, however, also be a serious financial headache if not handled in the correct way. If you let your debts pile up, they can harm your ability to get credit and loans in the future.

Using credit to your advantage can make your life much easier in many ways. Credit cards can help you build good credit and are great for use in some emergency situations when cash isn't available. Loans can help you pay for large purchases like cars, homes, and college education, when you wouldn't be able to pay for these things on your own.

If you rely too much on using credit and borrowed money, however, credit and debt can become a kind of financial trap. One of the main dangers of credit is the risk of taking on too much debt. People sometimes view credit cards as ways to stretch their incomes, to spend more money than they really have. This viewpoint leads to trouble!

In fact, credit cards are an invitation to use money more responsibly. It's up to you to know how much of your credit card bill you are able to pay off each month. Spending more than that can mean your debt holds over for next month. Too many months of this kind of spending, and your debt can become more than you can manage.

Some people even choose to use one credit card to pay off another. This can become a slippery slope toward high levels of debt, poor credit history, and a low credit score. Making sure to keep your credit card balances low and pay off your cards on time are important in avoiding growing debt.

Sticking to your loan repayment plans as well is also vital to managing your loan debts effectively, a key to avoiding the pitfalls of large debts.

Without a good credit history, you may miss out on some of life's opportunities. It will be much harder to take out a loan or get low interest rates on new credit cards. This makes it harder to purchase a house, attend college, or buy a car. Ultimately, the danger of debt is that it can lead to a cycle in which debts are never fully paid and your credit score goes down.

Using credit and borrowing money can be very helpful, but neither of these financial choices comes without consequences. Borrowing responsibly, which includes paying back all of your debts on time and in full, can help you avoid the more negative consequences that come with unpaid credit and loan debts!

WHAT IF YOU HAVE BAD CREDIT?

You know it's important to have good credit, but what can you do if you already have bad credit? Don't worry—there are many different ways for you to improve your credit over time.

Often, bad credit is the result of difficulty paying off debts. If you are having a hard time making payments on any kind of debt, whether from a loan or credit card, one of the best ways to get back on track is by contacting your lenders or creditors. In many cases, lenders will work with you to set up a payment plan that works better for your financial situation. Sticking to this kind of a payment schedule can help you reduce the amount of debt you have, which in turn improves your credit.

If, after contacting your lenders and working out a new payment plan, you are still having trouble making payments on time, it may be a good idea to contact a credit counseling service. Credit counselors are financial professionals who can assist you in coming up with a debt repayment plan that will be easy for you to stick with. When working with a credit counselor or counseling service, you must agree to make payments on time and in full. You'll pay the counseling service and they will work out paying your lenders or creditors.

Beyond getting help to make payments on your debts in order to improve your credit, you can also work to improve your credit score over time by getting your balances paid down on all your credit cards. By taking steps to increase your credit score and better your credit history, you are improving your financial outlook for the future.

Raising Your Credit Score

With all of the different ways that you can worsen your credit score, it may seem like bad credit is inevitable or inescapable, but that is far from the case. Not only do you have control over your credit history, but even if you have bad credit, it's easy enough to make things right and improve your score.

BAD CREDIT

Raising your score is actually easier than you might think. While you can't raise your score immediately—doing so takes a bit of work on your part—you can raise your credit score in what is a reasonably short period of time. In fact, the way that your credit score is calculated benefits you when you are trying to change your credit for the better. The formula used to calculate credit score is weighted so that more recent activity is given more importance. This means that, while you may not have perfect credit right now, if you are taking steps to lower your score—doing things like paying all of your bills on time, making sure your credit card balances are low, and making debt payments on time—you will be seen as improving. Rather than being defined by your past credit history, no matter how bad it is, you are defined by your most recent actions. Even a few months of improved credit habits can give the impression to lenders and others that you are cleaning up your act when it comes to credit cards, debt payments, and borrowing. Progress in the right direction, toward better managing your spending and credit, means a lot to lenders.

Remember, your credit score is merely a reflection of the way you use credit, and it can be improved. Your credit score isn't ever permanent, no matter how low. Raising your credit score takes time, but will be worth it in the end, when your good credit allows you to take out the loans you need to pay for the things you want in life, whether a car, a house, or an education.

Living Without Credit Stress

Making sure that your credit is good, and that it stays that way, can seem like an overwhelming challenge. Many young people can find dealing with credit—and finances in general—stressful, even so much so that they don't want to deal with it at all. But putting off facing credit debt just makes things worse! While you refuse to think about it, interest keeps accumulating, and your payments get later.

Understanding the issues surrounding credit—including how to best use credit, how it can be dangerous, and what lenders look for in your credit history—is often the first step toward making credit managable. Remember, your finances should never control you. You always have the power over your money and your credit. The goal is to take the steps necessary in order to make sure that credit is a tool for you to use, not something that makes your life harder. Credit exists to help you pay for some of the largest decisions in your life, not to run your life. By being aware of how credit works, you can make it work for you!

Here's What You Need to Remember

- Credit is essentially borrowed money. When you use a credit card or take out a loan, you are agreeing that you will borrow money now and pay it back later. Credit gives you the opportunity to pay for larger purchases over time, rather than all at once. By taking out a loan on a house or car for instance, you can pay for these larger items bit by bit each month.

- In addition to helping you make larger purchases, you need to use credit in order to build up a credit history. Lenders use your credit history to decide whether or not you can pay back a loan. If you have a good credit history, it means you're a responsible borrower, and that lenders can be sure you'll pay them back in full and on time.

- In order to establish a good credit history, you'll need to make sure to pay your rent and bills on time, and keep your debts low. Paying off your debts is the best way to maintain good credit.

- If you have poor credit, you'll have a harder time borrowing money. Lenders will be able to see whether or not you've used credit responsibly and make their lending decsions based on that information. Paying off your debts can help improve your credit.

- Although credit can be a great tool, having poor credit can limit the choices you can make in your life. Making sure to keep your credit debts low and make payments on time can insure that you keep good credit once you have it.

Words You Need to Know

balance: The amount of money in your bank account.

bankruptcy: The state of being unable to pay all your debts, and having to give up all your assets in order to pay your creditors.

budget: Assigning money for specific purposes in order to stay within your income.

consumers: People who buy and take advantage of economic goods and services.

creditors: People to whom a debt is owed.

debt: Money that is owed to someone else.

defer: To put off or delay.

dispute: To argue over.

foreclosed: A home that has been reclaimed by the bank because the owner is unable to make mortgage payments on it.

insurance: A way of guaranteeing safety or monetary security in the case of accident or unforeseen damage.

interest: A percentage of money borrowed that is owed to the lender.

intermediaries: Mediators or go-betweens.

mortgages: Agreements with banks or lending agencies that offer them homes as collateral against borrowing the price of said home.

overdraft: To take out more money than is in your bank account.

priorities: To put certain things—like food or rent—over other, less important ones—such as music or new clothes.

Further Reading

Allman, Barbara. *Banking*. Minneapolis, Minn.: Lerner, 2006.

Butler, Tamsen. *The Complete Guide to Personal Finance: For Teenagers and College Students*. Ocala, Fla.: Atlantic Publishing Group, 2010.

Byers, Ann. *First Credit Cards and Credit Smarts*. New York: Rosen Publishing, 2009.

Green, Meg. *Everything You Need to Know About Credit Cards and Fiscal Responsibility.* New York: Rosen Publishing, 2000.

Larson, Jennifer S. *Where Do We Keep Money? How Banks Work*. Minneapolis, Minn.: Lerner Classroom, 2010.

Weiss, Anne. *Easy Credit*. Minneapolis, Minn.: Millbrook Press, 2000.

find out more on the internet

"Credit and Charge Cards: What Consumers Should Know About the Cost and Terms of Credits"
Federal Reserve Bank of San Francico
www.frbsf.org/publications/consumer/cards.html

"How to Establish, Use, and Protect Your Credit"
Federal Reserve Bank of San Francico
www.frbsf.org/publications/consumer/credit.html

"Money 101—Financial Advice and Lessons Made Easy"
CNN Money
money.cnn.com/magazines/moneymag/money101

MyMoney
www.mymoney.gov

Young Money Magazine
www.youngmoney.com

The websites listed on this page were active at the time of publication. The publisher is not responsible for websites that have changed their address or discontinued operation since the date of publication. The publisher will review and update the websites upon each reprint.

Index

Photo Credits

About the Author and Consultant

Helen Thompson lives in upstate New York. She worked first as a social worker and then became a teacher as her second career. She taught money management skills to students in grades seven and eight for several years.

Brigitte Madrian is Professor of Public Policy and Corporate Management in the Aetna Chair at Harvard University's Kennedy School of Government. She has also been on the faculty at the Wharton School and the University of Chicago. She is also a Research Associate at the National Bureau of Economic Research and coeditor of the *Journal of Human Resources*. She is the first-place recipient of the National Academy of Social Insurance Dissertation Prize and the TIAA-CREF Paul A. Samuelson Award for Scholarly Research on Lifelong Financial Security.